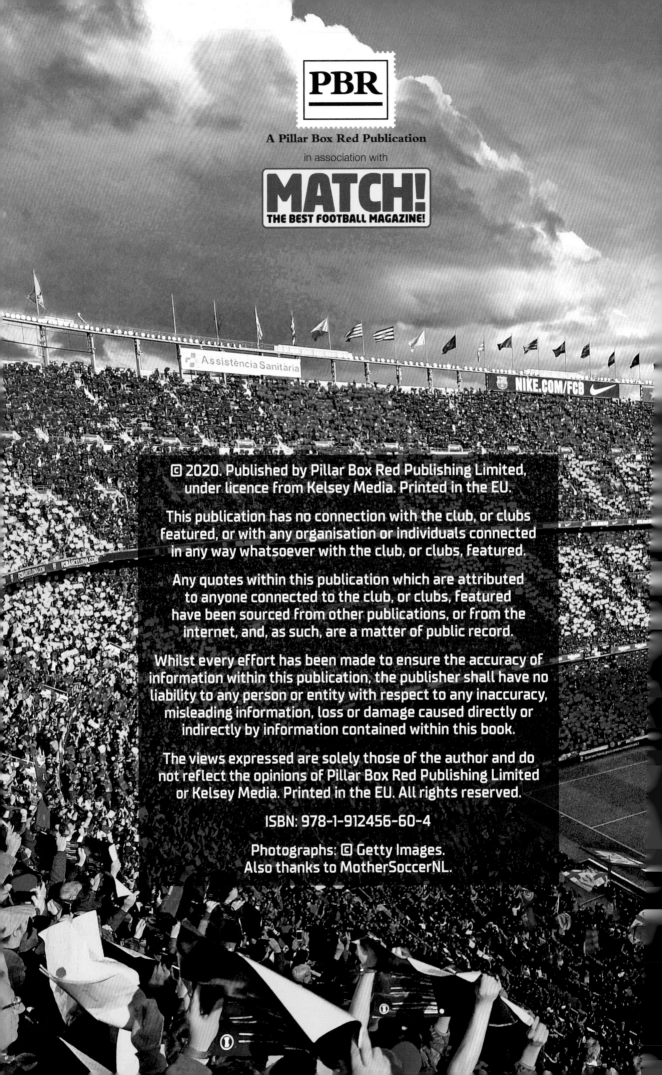

PBR

A Pillar Box Red Publication

in association with

MATCH!
THE BEST FOOTBALL MAGAZINE!

ISBN: 978-1-912456-60-4

Photographs: © Getty Images.
Also thanks to MotherSoccerNL.

BARCELONA ANNUAL 2021

Written by
Jared Tinslay

Edited by
Stephen Fishlock

Designed by
Darryl Tooth

CONTENTS

SEASON REVIEW

We look back at BARCA's 2019-20 campaign month by month, checking out their big moments, star players and tons more!

AUGUST

MEGA MOMENTS!

Barcelona stars training

There was bad news before the season even started for Barcelona – star player Lionel Messi injured his calf in pre-season training, and was ruled out for the start of a La Liga campaign for the first time in a decade! To make matters worse, they then lost their opening match of the season to Athletic Bilbao after a jaw-dropping Aritz Aduriz scissor-kick!

Griezmann off the mark

Blaugrana fans were in a much more positive mood after seeing their new signing Antoine Griezmann score a brace on his Nou Camp debut against Real Betis – and then highly-rated 16-year-old wonderkid Ansu Fati making his La Liga debut off the bench!

The month ended in really disappointing fashion, despite Fati scoring his first La Liga goal, with Ernesto Valverde's team letting a lead slip against an Osasuna side that they were expected to beat comfortably. Gerard Pique was at fault, with the Barca centre-back's handball in the area gifting their opponents a late penalty to equalise!

Fati celebrates

MAN OF THE MONTH!

ANSU FATI Nobody had really heard of Guinea-Bissau-born Fati before he impressed off the bench against Real Betis! He showed no fear again versus Osasuna, and marked the occasion by becoming Barcelona's youngest-ever scorer at senior level and the third-youngest scorer in La Liga history!

DID YOU KNOW?

Barcelona's shock defeat to rivals Athletic Bilbao at the San Mames was their first loss on the opening weekend of a La Liga season for 11 years. Ouch!

BARCELONA'S RESULTS

16/08	LIGA	Athletic Bilbao	1-0	Barcelona
25/08	LIGA	Barcelona	5-2	Real Betis
31/08	LIGA	Osasuna	2-2	Barcelona

SEPTEMBER
MEGA MOMENTS!

Fati scores again

Messi was finally ready to start his first game of the 2019-20 season against Villarreal, but was forced off through injury at half-time on his 400th La Liga start for the club! Luckily, La Blaugrana were still able to hold on to a narrow win!

High-fives all round

Wonderkid Fati marked his first senior start for Barcelona with a goal in the second minute against Valencia! He then turned assister for La Blaugrana's second goal, just five minutes later, setting up another high-scoring home victory!

Ter Stegen bossing it

Barcelona's Champions League campaign kicked off with a tough trip to Dortmund! They were lucky to return to Spain with a point, thanks to Marc-Andre ter Stegen's penalty save and a few point-blank range stops!

MAN OF THE MONTH!

MARC-ANDRE TER STEGEN Ter Stegen's display against Dortmund alone could have been enough to win the MOTM, but he also provided an amazing assist for Luis Suarez in the game against Getafe, which turned the tide in Barcelona's favour!

DID YOU KNOW?

Ter Stegen made it four saves out of six Champions League penalties faced after he stopped Borussia Dortmund forward Marco Reus' effort. Wow!

BARCELONA'S RESULTS

Date	Comp	Home	Score	Away
14/09	LIGA	Barcelona	5-2	Valencia
17/09	CL	B. Dortmund	0-0	Barcelona
21/09	LIGA	Granada	2-0	Barcelona
24/09	LIGA	Barcelona	2-1	Villarreal
28/09	LIGA	Getafe	0-2	Barcelona

OCTOBER
MEGA MOMENTS!

Suarez at the double

Barcelona were on a 32-game unbeaten home run in the Champions League before their match v Inter, but Lautaro Martinez threated to pour ice over that hot streak after scoring in the second minute! Luis Suarez saved the day with a fine double though, as he put Barca back in pole position in Group F!

Suarez was at it again in the La Liga clash with Sevilla – he scored a stunning overhead kick to open the scoring! Messi then finally got off the mark for 2019-20 with a delightful free-kick late on, before Ousmane Dembele and Ronald Araujo were both sent off!

Araujo sees red

Messi magic

The fans at the Nou Camp were treated to tons of net-busters in 2019-20, including five against Real Valladolid! Messi scored two and provided two assists as Barcelona returned to the top of the La Liga table!

MAN OF THE MONTH!

LIONEL MESSI Leo became the first-ever player to score in 15 consecutive Champions League seasons as Barcelona won away at Slavia Prague, while his curled free-kick against Valladolid was the 50th set-piece goal of his awesome career!

DID YOU KNOW?

The victory over Eibar was the first-ever game that Messi, Griezmann and Suarez all busted net in!

BARCELONA'S RESULTS

Date	Comp	Home	Score	Away
02/10	CL	Barcelona	2-1	Inter
06/10	LIGA	Barcelona	4-0	Sevilla
19/10	LIGA	Eibar	0-3	Barcelona
23/10	CL	Slavia Prague	1-2	Barcelona
29/10	LIGA	Barcelona	5-1	Real Valladolid

NOVEMBER
MEGA MOMENTS!

Treble for Leo

For the second time in his jaw-dropping career, Barcelona legend Messi completed a hat-trick full of set-pieces! He kicked things off with a penalty against Celta Vigo, before scoring two flaming free-kicks either side of the half-time whistle to guarantee Barcelona the three points!

BARCELONA'S RESULTS

02/11	LIGA	Levante	3-1	Barcelona
05/11	CL	Barcelona	0-0	Slavia Prague
09/11	LIGA	Barcelona	4-1	Celta Vigo
23/11	LIGA	Leganes	1-2	Barcelona
27/11	CL	Barcelona	3-1	B. Dortmund

Los Cules sealed their place in the knockout rounds of the Champions League with a dominant victory over Borussia Dortmund at the Nou Camp! On his 700th Barcelona appearance, Messi scored once and grabbed two assists in another virtuoso display!

Messi too hot to handle

MAN OF THE MONTH!
LIONEL MESSI It couldn't be anyone else but 'La Pulga'! He scored or assisted eight goals in just five matches in November, only failing to make his mark on the game against Slavia Prague – although he did hit the bar and have six shots on target!

DID YOU KNOW?
Their 0-0 draw with Slavia Prague was the first time in 46 home games that Barcelona had failed to bust net – and the first time that Messi had failed to score or assist in a CL home game since 2012!

DECEMBER
MEGA MOMENTS!

Atletico Madrid's awesome Wanda Metropolitano is one of the hardest places to visit in Europe, so Barcelona always have their work cut out there! It took a moment of magic from Messi – a sweetly curled strike from the edge of the area – to beat keeper Jan Oblak and win Barcelona the points!

Messi does it again

BARCELONA'S RESULTS

01/12	LIGA	Atletico Madrid	0-1	Barcelona
07/12	LIGA	Barcelona	5-2	Real Mallorca
10/12	CL	Inter	1-2	Barcelona
14/12	LIGA	Real Sociedad	2-2	Barcelona
18/12	LIGA	Barcelona	0-0	Real Madrid
21/12	LIGA	Barcelona	4-1	Alaves

El Clasico stalemate

The first El Clasico of the 2019-20 season had loads of pre-match hype, but the game massively failed to deliver. It was one of the dullest derbies MATCH had seen in seasons, but meant Barcelona stayed top of La Liga on goal difference going into 2020!

MAN OF THE MONTH!
LIONEL MESSI In the month that he was handed a record-breaking sixth Ballon d'Or award, Messi was majestic once more! On top of his goal against Atletico, he hit a hat-trick against Mallorca and his 50th goal of 2019 with a fine finish against Alaves!

DID YOU KNOW?
Teenager Ansu Fati became the youngest goalscorer in Champions League history after busting net just a minute after coming off the bench against Inter!

JANUARY

MEGA MOMENTS!

For the first time ever, the Spanish Super Cup took a new format, with Barcelona facing Atletico Madrid in a semi-final in Saudi Arabia! It was an action-packed match, with Barcelona throwing away a 2-1 lead to lose 3-2 late on!

Barca sunk by Atleti

BARCELONA'S RESULTS

04/01	LIGA	Espanyol	2-2	Barcelona
09/01	SUC	Barcelona	2-3	Atletico Madrid
19/01	LIGA	Barcelona	1-0	Granada
22/01	CDR	Ibiza	1-2	Barcelona
25/01	LIGA	Valencia	2-0	Barcelona
30/01	CDR	Barcelona	5-0	Leganes

Days after losing that clash to Atletico Madrid, Barcelona bosses decided to make their first mid-season managerial change since 2003 – sacking Ernesto Valverde and bringing in ex-Real Betis coach Quique Setien!

Setien arrives

Grizi punches the air

Barcelona ended the month in strong fashion, thrashing Leganes 5-0 to reach the quarter-finals of the Copa del Rey – a competition they've won a record 30 times! Lionel Messi scored a brace in what was his 500th win in a Barcelona shirt!

MAN OF THE MONTH!

ANTOINE GRIEZMANN As well as scoring against his old club Atletico for the first time in the Spanish Super Cup, Grizi also busted net twice against Ibiza to complete a comeback in the Copa del Rey – and got the opening goal in that thrashing of Leganes!

DID YOU KNOW?

Barcelona's draw with Espanyol continued their unbeaten run against their city rivals – they haven't lost in the league against them since 2009!

FEBRUARY

MEGA MOMENTS!

Barca protest during the Bilbao defeat

Just like back in August in the league, Barcelona suffered a last-minute defeat to Athletic Bilbao to knock them out of the Copa del Rey – although this time it took an injury-time own goal from defensive midfielder Sergio Busquets to settle the result!

BARCELONA'S RESULTS

02/02	LIGA	Barcelona	2-1	Levante
06/02	CDR	Athletic Bilbao	1-0	Barcelona
09/02	LIGA	Real Betis	2-3	Barcelona
15/02	LIGA	Barcelona	2-1	Getafe
22/02	LIGA	Barcelona	5-0	Eibar
25/02	CL	Napoli	1-1	Barcelona

Braithwaite unveiling

After Ousmane Dembele was ruled out for six months, La Liga gave Barcelona special permission to sign a striker outside of the transfer window – and they moved to sign Leganes' Martin Braithwaite for £15 million!

The quarter-finals of the Champions League saw Barca drawn against Serie A side Napoli, with the first leg played in Italy. Dries Mertens put the home side ahead, before Antoine Griezmann latched on to a Nelson Semedo cross to score an important away goal!

Griezmann on target

MAN OF THE MONTH!

LIONEL MESSI In another mind-boggling month, Argentina magician Messi was directly involved in ten of Barcelona's 12 league goals – he grabbed six assists and scored four goals of his own! All four of his net-busters came against Eibar, with his opener a crazy chipped finish over the keeper!

DID YOU KNOW?

Centre-back Clement Lenglet scored the winner and was sent off in Barca's thrilling away win v Real Betis!

MARCH

MEGA MOMENTS!

Vinicius Jr. reels away in celebration

Camp Nou in lockdown

Football was interrupted in mid-March due to the coronavirus pandemic, with La Liga and lots of other leagues across the world having to postpone or cancel their seasons entirely!

El Clasico rivals Real Madrid got the upper hand in the La Liga title race with a solid 2-0 win over Barca at the Santiago Bernabeu, thanks to goals from Vinicius Jr. and Mariano Diaz!

Leo spot on

A week after their Clasico defeat, Barcelona got back on track with a win over Real Sociedad – Messi scoring the only goal from the penalty spot! Real Madrid lost to Real Betis to put Barca back on top!

MAN OF THE MONTH!

MARTIN BRAITHWAITE Messi might have scored the winning penalty in the clash against Sociedad, but he actually had a bad game by his ridiculously high standards. Denmark forward Braithwaite was Man of the Match and was starting to prove that he could be a useful signing for La Blaugrana!

DID YOU KNOW?

Their El Clasico defeat in March marked the first time since 1974-75 that Barca had failed to score a single goal v Real Madrid in a league season!

BARCELONA'S RESULTS

Date		Home	Score	Away
01/03	LIGA	Real Madrid	2-0	Barcelona
07/03	LIGA	Barcelona	1-0	Real Sociedad

JUNE

MEGA MOMENTS!

Speedy start by Vidal

Football restarted with a bang for Barcelona! In their first game back after lockdown, Los Cules thrashed Mallorca 4-0, going ahead after just 65 seconds thanks to an Arturo Vidal header!

Aspas denies Barca

The matches came thick and fast in June, but Barca looked like they were starting to tire by the end of the month. They threw-away a 2-1 lead against Celta Vigo, conceding a late sucker-punch!

Things went from bad to worse when they met Atletico Madrid three days after that Celta Vigo draw. Barca went ahead twice, but still couldn't record a win – giving Real a big advantage in the title race!

Barca slip up again

BARCELONA'S RESULTS

Date		Home	Score	Away
13/06	LIGA	Real Mallorca	0-4	Barcelona
16/06	LIGA	Barcelona	2-0	Leganes
19/06	LIGA	Sevilla	0-0	Barcelona
23/06	LIGA	Barcelona	1-0	Athletic Bilbao
27/06	LIGA	Celta Vigo	2-2	Barcelona
30/06	LIGA	Barcelona	2-2	Atletico Madrid

MAN OF THE MONTH!

LIONEL MESSI Messi became the first player ever to score 20 La Liga goals in 12 consecutive seasons with his awesome strike against Mallorca, and then chipped a cheeky Panenka penalty past Atletico Madrid goalkeeper Jan Oblak to mark his 700th career goal for club and country. Take a bow, Leo!

DID YOU KNOW?

Ansu Fati became the second-youngest player ever to score five La Liga goals when he fired home in the 4-0 away win against struggling Mallorca!

JULY

MEGA MOMENTS!

Title hopes dashed

Barca's dreams of winning the La Liga title were over after they suffered a shock defeat at home to ten-man Osasuna! It meant rivals Real Madrid were able to lift their first league trophy since 2017!

Messi bags the Golden Boot

Even though they'd lost out in the title race, Barca made sure they ended the league season on a high – they thrashed Alaves 5-0, with Messi winning his fourth La Liga Golden Boot in a row!

Griezmann masterclass v Villarreal

Antoine Griezmann produced his best performance of the campaign in Barca's 4-1 victory over Villarreal – including scoring one of the best goals of the 2019-20 La Liga season! He hit a 20-yard chip over the goalkeeper's head to put Barcelona 3-1 ahead!

BARCELONA'S RESULTS

05/07	LIGA	Villarreal	1-4	Barcelona
08/07	LIGA	Barcelona	1-0	Espanyol
11/07	LIGA	Real Valladolid	0-1	Barcelona
16/07	LIGA	Barcelona	1-2	Osasuna
19/07	LIGA	Alaves	0-5	Barcelona

MAN OF THE MONTH!

LIONEL MESSI In typically mind-boggling fashion, the unplayable Barca forward ended the seventh month of the year with seven goals and assists combined! As well as bagging a record-breaking seventh all-time La Liga Golden Boot, he also finished the campaign with 21 assists – an all-time Spanish league record for a single season. Hero!

DID YOU KNOW?

Messi's former Barcelona team-mate Xavi held the previous record for most assists in a single season when he grabbed 20 back in 2008-09!

AUGUST

MEGA MOMENTS!

Barca edge out Napoli

Bayern's Coutinho scores v his parent club

Barcelona travelled to Lisbon, Portugal, to face an in-form Bayern Munich side in the Champions League quarter-finals – the German giants had just beaten Chelsea 7-1 on aggregate in the last 16! A crazy first half saw Bayern lead 4-1 at half-time, and things just got embarrassing after the break!

Barcelona's Champions League campaign finally resumed in August with a busy second-leg victory over Italian side Napoli. All four of the game's goals were scored in the first half, including a mazy run and finish from Messi and a Luis Suarez penalty!

BARCELONA'S RESULTS

08/08	CL	Barcelona	3-1	Napoli
14/08	CL	Barcelona	2-8	Bayern Munich

MAN OF THE MONTH!

LIONEL MESSI Napoli were the 35th victims of a Messi Champions League goal – he's scored against more CL opponents than any other player! He was Man of the Match against the Italians, but still saw the season end in the worst possible way v Bayern!

DID YOU KNOW?

Barcelona qualified for the Champions League quarter-finals for the 13th consecutive campaign – the longest run in the tournament's history!

TER STEGEN

SOLID SHOT-STOPPER

The Germany goalkeeper is the definition of a sweeper keeper!

For an outsider looking in, it might be a surprise to see goalkeeper Marc-Andre ter Stegen with two assists to his name in the club's 2019-20 La Liga stats charts – sitting above the likes of Ansu Fati, Ousmane Dembele and Martin Braithwaite – but, for anyone associated with the club, it's no huge shock. As Antoine Griezmann mentioned, after scoring from a perfectly executed ter Stegen long ball last season, "Marc is incredible – he's good with his feet and like a midfielder for us." Indeed, the solid goalkeeper positions himself in such a way that he's always open to receive the ball from his teammates – and that's a key reason the team are able to play the tiki-taka tactics so important to fans...

UNUSUAL BEGINNINGS

Ter Stegen's past helps explain a little bit about why he's so at ease with the ball at his feet. He grew up in Monchengladbach, Germany, and was signed up for local side Borussia Monchengladbach by his grandfather when he was just four years old. Interestingly enough, he actually started out playing as a striker for his youth team, before being asked to take over from an injured goalkeeper when he was ten. Thankfully for Barca, he never looked back!

MILESTONE MARCH

Ter Stegen has already set one record by becoming the first Barcelona goalkeeper in the 21st century to register an assist, but he's heading towards another important milestone – reaching the club's top five for most matches played by a goalkeeper. He should move into the top six by the end of 2020-21, and another three injury-free seasons could see him move into third spot – just behind all-time club legends Victor Valdes and Andoni Zubizarreta!

SUPERSTITIOUS SIP

Footballers are known for adopting strange superstitions for good luck on the pitch – and that obviously goes for goalkeepers too! One thing we've noticed ter Stegen likes to do is have a sip from his water bottle every time Barca score a goal. We can only imagine that when La Blaugrana hammered Huesca 8-2 back in the 2018-19 season, the keeper must have spent most of the game desperately looking towards the changing room toilets!

INTERNATIONAL PATIENCE

Believe it or not, ter Stegen has never played a game at one of football's major international tournaments – neither the Euros nor the World Cup. With Bayern Munich legend Manuel Neuer the country's first-choice goalkeeper for over a decade, ter Stegen has had to settle for a place on the bench. The battle to be the nation's No.1 is a constant talking point among fans, but Barcelona supporters will be backing their man for the upcoming Euros!

FACTPACK

Position: Goalkeeper
Country: Germany
D.O.B: 30/04/1992
Height: 6ft 2in
Boots: adidas Predator
Instagram: @mterstegen1

BARCELONA BRAIN-BUSTER!

How well do you know the Catalan club?

1. Which La Liga rivals did Barcelona sign goalkeeper Neto from in 2019?

2. True or False? Jose Mourinho used to work as an interpreter for the club!

3. Who did Barca Femeni beat 10-1 in the 2020 Super Cup Final – Betis, Sociedad or Valladolid?

4. What was the main colour of the club's cool third kit in 2019-20 – green or yellow?

5. What was the aggregate score of the La Liga Clasicos in 2019-20?

6. What year did goalkeeper Marc-Andre ter Stegen join Los Cules – 2013, 2014 or 2015?

7. Name the ex-Barcelona legend who was captain before Lionel Messi!

8. Which English side did Martin Braithwaite used to play for – Leeds or Middlesbrough?

9. Who scored more league goals in 2019-20 – Antoine Griezmann or Luis Suarez?

10. Is Quique Setien older or younger than former Barca boss Ernesto Valverde?

1 ....
2 ....
3 ....
4 ....
5 ....
6 ....
7 ....
8 ....
9 ....
10 ....

WORDFIT

Fit 25 of the club's all-time top goalscorers into the huge grid!

Alcantara	Eto'o	Kubala	Pedro	Saviola
Amor	Henry	Lineker	Rivaldo	Stoichkov
Cesar	Iniesta	Martin	Ronaldinho	Suarez
Enrique	Kluivert	Messi	Ronaldo	Villa
Escola	Koeman	Neymar	Samitier	Xavi

ANSWERS ON PAGE 60

NEW CAMP
IN NUMBERS!

Check out all the amazing facts behind Barcelona's future stadium

5,646
The capacity increase from what it stands at currently!

12,000
A 12,000-seat indoor basketball arena is also being built near the site!

3
There will be three ring-shaped tiers around the whole ground!

105,000
The future capacity once the redevelopment is complete!

6,000
The plans also included a new 6,000-capacity stadium for their B team, which is already in use!

The cool new roof will have rainwater collectors, which funnels through into the on-pitch sprinkler system!

NOU

£520M
Estimated cost of expanding the current Camp Nou facilities!

2019
The year the stadium renovation project began!

2023
The year the new stadium is expected to be ready!

360
Each tier will have a 360-degree walkway with views of the city!

47,000
The ground will have a new 47,000m² roof to protect fans from rain and raise sound levels!

The ultra revolutionary stadium will also harvest solar energy and use it to help grow the grass on the pitch!

LEO MESSI
LIVING LEGEND

The Argentina forward will be a Blaugrana icon forever!

The making of a global megastar doesn't come easy, and Messi might not have been the player he is today if it wasn't for the backing of Barcelona. When he was just ten years old, he was diagnosed with a growth hormone deficiency, threatening his future as a professional footballer. His club in Argentina, Newell's Old Boys, couldn't afford the medical fees, but Barcelona saw enough talent in him during a trial to offer him a place in La Masia – with the treatment fees included. Throughout his career, he's transformed from a scrawny teenage sensation, nicknamed 'The Flea', into what many fans and footy experts consider to be 'The Goat' – the greatest footballer of all time. And MATCH tends to agree...

LA LIGA LEGEND

Since making his La Liga debut as a 17-year-old in October 2004 v city rivals Espanyol, Messi has gone on to break all sorts of Spanish league records. He's made more La Liga appearances than any other non-Spanish star, recorded more wins than any other player, grabbed an all-time record number of assists, goals and hat-tricks, and won more La Liga Best Player awards than any other person in history. We could go on, but we'd another entire annual!

GOAL MACHINE

Ask any football fan what Messi's best attribute is: some will say dribbling, while others will mention vision, some his passing, and others his goalscoring – that's what proves he's such a fantastic all-round player! We're shouting out to his finishing, though – no player has won more European Golden Shoes than Messi's six, while his 92 goals in 2012 is the most any player has ever scored in a calendar year. We doubt anyone will ever match that record, either!

MESSI: THE BRAND

Argentina's all-time top scorer has built an impressive brand through his playing career – he was named the world's highest-paid athlete in the world in 2019! As well as appearing on numerous FIFA and Pro Evolution Soccer covers, he's also an adidas athlete with his own Nemeziz colourways, has a Messi Store clothing range and over 150m followers on Instagram! In 2019, he even had a circus in Barcelona to celebrate his amazing career and skills!

THE GOAT

For the last decade, football fans across the world have debated whether Cristiano Ronaldo or Lionel Messi is the better player but, for many footy experts, that contest ended in December 2019. The two rivals were level on five Ballons d'Or each – the prize awarded to the best footballer in the world – before Messi was named winner of the 2019 vote. That took him to six in total – more than any other star in history – giving bragging rights to Messi followers!

FACTPACK

Position: Forward
Country: Argentina
D.O.B: 24/06/1987
Height: 5ft 7In
Boots: adidas Nemeziz
Instagram: @leomessi

'10'1 THINGS YOU NEED TO KNOW ABOUT... BARCELONA

1 Lionel Messi is the club's all-time top goalscorer in all comps with over 630 official goals!

2 Barcelona have won a record 12 Ballon d'Or awards with the likes of Ronaldinho, Rivaldo, Johan Cruyff and Messi all getting their hands on it!

3 Barcelona Femeni are the only Spanish side to reach the final of the Champions League!

5 Messi's full name is Lionel Andres Messi Cuccittini!

4 Barca's club crest from 1910 is almost identical to the one they still have today!

6 Legendary midfielder Xavi is the club's all-time record appearance maker, although Messi is creeping up on him!

7 Barcelona were founded way back in October 1899 by a group of Swiss, Spanish, German and English footballers!

8 Their founder, Joan Gamper, placed an advert in a local newspaper asking for more players to join his new team!

9 Football experts reckon Barcelona's iconic kit colours come from a rugby team for whom two of the club's English members had played for previously!

10 Other theorists reckon the colours actually come from Gamper's favourite Swiss side – FC Basel!

11 The club crest was originally the same as Barcelona's city badge, but they designed their own in 1910!

12 The top half of the badge contains the St. George's Cross on the left side, which represents the patron saint of Catalonia, and the Catalan flag on the right!

13 The ball in the lower middle of the crest represents Barca's desire to play attractive, possession football!

14 There are five values that define the spirit of the club – respect, effort, ambition, humility and teamwork!

15 The values go hand-in-hand with the club's motto 'Mes Que Un Club' – or 'More Than A Club', in English!

16 That iconic motto came from a speech given by former Barcelona president Narcis de Carreras in 1968!

17 The motto can also be found on the seats at the megaclub's jaw-dropping Camp Nou stadium!

18 Another key element to the Barcelona identity is their world-famous club hymn that echoes around the stands on match days!

19 The hymn is officially called 'El Cant del Barca', and was composed in 1974 to celebrate the club's 75th anniversary!

20 The hymn is played through loudspeakers before and after every match at the Camp Nou!

21 Barca won their first-ever trophy back in 1902 – the Copa Macaya – which was contested between Catalan clubs!

22 The year 1902 was also the first-ever Clasico – and Barcelona beat rivals Real Madrid 3-1 in the Spanish capital!

23 Real Madrid actually scored the first goal in that debut El Clasico, but it was the result that really mattered!

24 Barcelona opened a brand-new 22,000-capacity ground way back in 1922, which was called Camp de les Corts – or Les Corts, for short!

25 Les Corts was expanded in 1944, 1946 and again in 1950, increasing the capacity to around 60,000 fans!

26 Eventually, plans began on building an even bigger stadium, with work on the Camp Nou commencing in 1954!

27 The Camp Nou took three years to be built and was opened in 1957, with an initial capacity of 99,053 spectators!

28 The away dressing room is a basic white to avoid feeling welcoming!

29 The men's side have lifted the Champions League trophy five times – most recently in 2015!

Search player/team/league...

FC Barcelona
FIFA 20
Team Rating: ★ ★ ★ ★ ★
League: LaLiga Santander

Overall Rating	Attack Rating	Midfield Rating	Defence Rating
OVR 86	ATT 90	MID 85	8

30 Barcelona were the highest-rated team on FIFA 20, with 260 points overall!

31 In the very beginning, the club's shirt was half blue and half claret, with white shorts!

32 Unlike the away dressing room, the home changing room at the Camp Nou is painted in La Blaugrana's famous colours!

33 Today, the Camp Nou has a capacity of 99,354, making it the largest football stadium in the whole of Europe!

34 There's a small chapel beside the tunnel leading to the Camp Nou pitch!

36 In 2012-13, they finished 15 points ahead of runners-up Real Madrid – a record margin!

37 There's a statue of legendary ex-striker Laszlo Kubala outside the ground!

39 Barca have competed in 41 Copa del Rey finals – two more than Real Madrid!

40 Barcelona's 5-0 win over Sevilla in the 2018 final was a joint-record biggest winning margin!

35 Lionel Messi is La Liga's record scorer, and has bagged more goals in a single season than any other player – 50 net-busters in 2011-12!

38 In 1949, Barcelona won their first-ever European trophy – the Latin Cup, organised by FIFA!

41 There's a museum at the stadium with trophies on show and interactive screens!

42 The 2019-20 Copa del Rey campaign was the first time in seven seasons that Barcelona hadn't reached the final!

43 Lionel Messi has scored more Copa goals than any other current player!

44 The club won their first-ever La Liga trophy back in 1929 – the Spanish league's first season in history!

45 The Latin Cup was contested by the league champions of Spain, Portugal, Italy and France, with Barcelona edging out Sporting 2-1 in the 1949 final!

46 Their jaw-dropping team from the 1950s had lethal striker Laszlo Kubala, who once scored a La Liga record seven goals in one game!

47 Talking about records – Barcelona hold loads of them, starting with recording a joint-highest La Liga points tally of 100 in the 2012-13 season!

48 They've managed a 100% winning home record in four different campaigns – more than any other side!

49 Their 43 consecutive league games without defeat, between April 2017 and May 2018, is another amazing record!

50 They hold the record for the biggest ever away victory – they've won 8-0 on the road on four different occasions...

51 ...However they also hold the record for suffering the biggest away defeat – Athletic Bilbao hammered them 12-1 in 1931!

52 They've appeared in every single top-flight campaign in Spain, along with Real Madrid and Athletic Bilbao!

53 Another of their records is Lionel Messi being the highest goalscorer and top assister in El Clasico history!

54 Talking about El Clasico, Barca boast a better winning record than Real, with more all-time wins in all competitions!

55 The two teams have met more than 275 times in their long history, and played out some absolute crackers!

56 It was estimated that around 650 million people worldwide tuned in to watch their December 2017 clash!

57 Believe it or not, 39 different players have appeared for both Real Madrid and Barcelona over the years. Madness!

58 Of those 39 players, 23 moved from Barcelona to Real, and 16 vice versa!

59 Barcelona broke the world-record transfer fee to sign Dutch legend Johan Cruyff in 1973 for £922,000!

60 And the club shattered it again in 1996 to sign Brazilian goal machine Ronaldo from PSV Eindhoven for £13 million!

61 Barca have been involved in some world-record outgoings, too – none bigger than Brazil trickster Neymar's mad £198 million move to PSG in 2017!

62 As well as a football team, Barcelona also have beach soccer, handball, roller hockey, futsal and basketball teams!

63 The club's star-studded futsal team have won more Copas del Rey than any other club in the competition's history...

64 ...While their handball and roller hockey teams are the most successful in Spain and Europe, too!

65 Their football team from 1951-52 is known as the 'Barca of Five Cups', because they won all five trophies on offer!

66 Here's another Messi record alert – Leo's won more La Liga trophies than any non-Spanish player!

67 Before leaving the Camp Nou, Neymar was a big hit at Barcelona, scoring 105 goals in 186 matches between 2013 and 2017!

68 There were seven Barca stars in Spain's World Cup-winning squad – more than any other side!

70 Barcelona's epic La Masia academy can be translated into English as 'The Farmhouse'!

72 The Estadi Johan Cruyff holds 6,000 spectators, and was opened in August 2019 as part of the new Espai Barca. Class!

73 Barcelona's first team train at the Ciutat Esportiva, while the youth team play their matches there!

74 The famour 'MSN' attack, consisting of Messi, Suarez and Neymar, was one of the deadliest strikeforces of all time!

FC Barcelona
@fcbarcelona
Home
Shop
Posts
Videos
Photos
Live
About
Community
Events
Groups
Create a Page

69 When Diego Maradona joined from Boca Juniors for £5 million in 1982, it was also for a world-record transfer fee!

71 Barca have got a deal with Nike, who've been making their kits since 1998!

75 Luis Figo lost his legendary status when he left Barca to join Real Madrid for a world-record fee in 2000. Ouch!

76 The Barca brand is one of the biggest in the world – they've got over 200 million followers across their social media channels!

77 Only massive rivals Real Madrid can boast a bigger following on social media than La Blaugrana!

78 The official Barcelona YouTube channel has over 9.5 million subscribers and tons of epic videos!

79 Barcelona were ranked the world's richest club for the first time in their history in January 2020!

80 Barcelona's official club megastore sells kits, but also other things like soft toys, mugs and even baby dummies!

81 Barcelona supporters can pay to become official club members and then vote on important matters – like the club's next president. Cool!

82 Back in 2017–18, fans could get a season ticket for as little as £149...

83 ...But in 2019–20, the club were selling VIP season tickets for £170 a game!

84 Their old La Masia building used to house around 60 academy players at a time, but was replaced by the fancy new Ciutat Esportiva Joan Gamper in 2011!

85 The new building has 78 bedrooms and can house 83 athletes at a time!

86 There are five grass pitches and four artificial grass pitches at the complex, as well as a multisport arena!

87 The club are currently transforming the facilities and local area into a new state-of-the-art Espai Barca!

88 There's also an ice rink in the Barca grounds, with it being free for use for members with their own ice skates!

89 The iconic 2009 team won La Liga, the Champions League, Copa del Rey, UEFA Super Cup, Spanish Super Cup and FIFA Club World Cup. Glorious!

90 On top of that, La Masia product Pep Guardiola was in charge of the club for that trophy-laden campaign!

91 In 2014, under Luis Enrique, they also became the first-ever club to complete two European trebles!

92 Like fellow legends Pep Guardiola and Johan Cruyff, Luis Enrique was another manager to win La Liga at Barca as both a player and manager. Hero!

93 Andres Iniesta is one of just three players to be applauded by Real Madrid fans at the Santiago Bernabeu...

94 ...They were clapping him for scoring Spain's winner in the 2010 World Cup final – the nation's only ever victory!

95 Barcelona Femeni and the Barca B team both play at the Estadi Johan Cruyff, named after the club legend!

96 Barcelona Femeni won the Spanish Super Cup for the first time in 2020, hammering Real Sociedad 10–1 in the final!

97 Club legend Marta Torrejon scored four goals in that thrashing – two either side of the half-time whistle. Wow!

98 Eight of their starting XI from that victory were from Spain, with Caroline Graham Hansen, Lieke Martens and Asisat Oshoala the exceptions!

99 In 2010, Barca became the first club ever to have three academy players make the top three of the Ballon d'Or – Iniesta, Messi and Xavi!

100 The Barcelona women's team were founded in 1988, and have won five La Liga trophies in total!

101 Pep Guardiola remains the most successful manager in the club's history in terms of trophies won!

BARCA S

GRIEZMANN

Grizi is a giant fan of NBA – and even had a basketball court built at his house so he could practise!

SERGI ROBERTO

When Sergi was asked to pick a song that could make him cry, he chose Ed Sheeran's Thinking Out Loud!

VIDAL

The spikey-haired midfielder is a big fan of horse racing and has his own stables!

LENGLET

Lenglet's not very adventurous with his food – he eats a lot of rice and pasta, and his fave French food is cheese!

NETO

The substitute goalie's dad was also a goalkeeper – and the reason Neto wanted to be one!

BUSQUETS

Notifications

Messages

Bookmarks

Lists

Sergio Busquets ✓
@5sergiob

Cuenta oficial de Sergio Busquets | Jugador del FC Barcelona y de la Selección Española de Fútbol
Translate bio

📍 Barcelona, Spain 📅 Joined February 2019

33 Following   235.1K Followers

Not followed by anyone you're following

Tweets   Tweets & replies   Media

Sergio Busquets ✓ @5sergiob · May 6, 2019
#LFCBarça We're ready! 💪🔵🔴

The midfielder used to refuse to go on social media, but he finally caved in in 2019 and can be found on Instagram and Twitter!

TARS revealed!

ALBA

The rapid defender actually spent all of his childhood playing as a striker, before becoming a winger and then eventually a left-back!

TER STEGEN

The solid shot-stopper owns a scooter and has been spotted riding about on it in the city!

DE JONG

Frenkie visited the Camp Nou as a supporter back in 2015, and even owned a Barcelona shirt with Messi on the back as a child!

PIQUE

The CB's full-name is actually Gerard Pique Bernabeu – he shares his surname with their El Clasico rivals' stadium!

BRAITHWAITE

The striker used to have a massive Afro earlier in his career – you almost wouldn't recognise him!

PJANIC

New boy Miralem Pjanic is a real brainiac in the Barca dressing room – the class CM can speak six different languages!

FATI

The wonderkid's follower count on Instagram went from 55,000 to 475,000 after making his debut for the club. Wow!

WORDSEARCH

Can you find these Barcelona-related words in the grid below?

```
V W R E S P A N Y O L H B U C W C T B Y I P R S X B F Q L X
H L O I T E V W J X N W H H V Y A W U T D K M M X O S J J N
K D Z S O J N A T C O A Q H S B T W S E E C V Y G K X H R W
P Y Q Q M H G L L K U F F A X L A Y Q P H L I G U F H W N W
J A R C B J I D O D U L N E S H L B U M S L S Y A O N E D E
F X S W G L M I V D E A E V M Y A W E G N E C J R M V C P X
C Y U G Q M P C A R R S P S O E N N T W N V A L D A N V O G
H V N A H D T B Z G T G U H V Q N E S I T O R F I R H V Y D
X L Z Y U G L Q L D E G Y W L Q A I Q D E C O Q O A Z L M D
X V T T Q V W U N F R G O C W Z V P Q S K V I K L D X M U D
S D G K K E Z V M U N A L A G I Z P C M G G C N A O F K P R
J P H R Z A W O S E A C L A S I C O D N N U R S B N W D O J
T R R Z W D O N A N S J E G T D P J Z L G Z F P E A E F Z E
E N O D E N E S A I A S U Q I Q X C T A G I Q A D J B Q G A
S A V P L T G R N M G N I K M K Z R Y L Z B R I P P Q F S B
E X O N R U G F G M H D R N G X R C J I H M T N V M B A V Q
H F K A M U I C Y V Z D C B A I M Q S G W W X P F Q O D D V
Y Z M Q A K Y P J R W E R E R R M W K A C B O D G E D I R P
M F H L Y R L E I Q K S U K X Y A B U X K B D T E Z G J J F
N P B H S S D X V I Q X Y Q S I P L L I M L E Q R R A L U X
M A L V E S R T N A J P F O S I I S L T L C Q J J B T U Q J
B V B A Z F J Z S A G W F A D T Q T Q O U M U B M N P T U D
L A A G M W I M E Q M C M R M C U S I X D E A L L M M R I K
G A M P E R F D T N X A X X W X E O U L M K G N A W Y I N W
C G X T V J T G I U L F L F G B Q S G O V N T C F W Z J T J
A W X F U J R Y E P N R K A V I P J T E V L U V P A Y K U K
E O M Y P Y A Y N I P L O A U Q Z R V J B O N V N U R A P I
D R W E P K P Q O A I R M T D D A M N H N X B R K Z F A L W
D U G C P K S U O J U V I Q D B M U L N D I B G A Y Y R E Q
E Q H E I L C J D F E V Y Y I J W B D K Y J V Y M S D D U K
```

Alves	Clasico	Gamper	Martens	Quintuple
Azulgranas	Cruyff	Guardiola	Messi	Rijkaard
Bartomeu	Cules	Hymn	Nike	Setien
Blaugrana	Deco	La Liga	Nou Camp	Spain
Busquets	Espanyol	La Masia	Pique	Valdes
Catalan	Femeni	Maradona	Puyol	Visca

ACTION REPLAY

How much can you remember from Barcelona's 5-1 thrashing of Real Madrid back in 2018-19?

1 In which month was this El Clasico played – October or December?

2 Who replaced the injured Lionel Messi in attack – Rafinha, Ansu Fati or Malcom?

3 Name the Brazilian baller who scored the game's opener!

4 True or False? Luis Suarez's third goal of the game was a penalty!

5 What was the score at half-time – 1-0, 2-0, 3-0 or 4-0?

6 Which Real Madrid defender scored their only goal of the game – Marcelo or Sergio Ramos?

7 Arturo Vidal completed the rout, but did he score with his left foot, right foot or head?

8 Which El Clasico rival had more shots on goal in total?

9 True or False? Real boss Julen Lopetegui got sacked a day later!

ANSWERS ON PAGE 60

JORDI ALBA

FLYING FULL-BACK

The lightning-quick left-back still has pace to burn!

When people think about the perfect modern-day full-back, they imagine an attack-minded player who can influence the game in the opponent's half, but who also has the energy to quickly get back into shape and the defensive ability to stop attacks – and prime Jordi Alba was one of the best this planet's ever seen! Barcelona were the envy of Europe when they had the Spain left-back bombing down one flank and Dani Alves the other – they excelled in the club's convincing 2015 Champions League final victory over Juventus! With 1 trophies to his name already at Barca, the flying full-back will go down as a club legend when he eventually leaves the Camp Nou, but that won't be for a while just yet...

ONE WHO ALMOST GOT AWAY

Born in Catalonia, Alba started his career in the youth ranks at Barcelona as a forward in their famous La Masia academy. However, in 2005, the club decided to release him for being too small. He finished his football education at La Liga rivals Valencia, and turned heads during two impressive seasons for their first team. Eventually, Blaugrana bosses admitted their mistake and paid just under £10 million to bring Alba back to the Nou Camp in 2012!

THE MOTORCYCLE

The full-back's standout attribute has always been his incredible acceleration – it's been a devastating attacking weapon and defensive shield for Barcelona over the years. He soon earned the nickname 'El Moto' – or the Motorcycle, in English – for his ability to burn past opponents with his lightning speed, but an interesting fact about Alba is that he only got his driving licence last summer! Before that, he was often spotted getting a lift into training by his dad!

MAGIC MESSI CONNECTION

Some footballers are just made to play together – and Alba and Messi are a perfect example! Even though they operate in completely different areas and sides of the pitch, Alba has assisted Leo more times than any other Barcelona player – their on-pitch connection is out of this world! One of the most iconic Messi goals over the years has been a first-time finish from an Alba cutback – something that opponents have never been able to prevent!

Jordi Alba 2024

THREE MORE YEARS

The defender's importance to the club was highlighted in February 2019 – less than a month before his 30th birthday. He was handed a new five-year contract, with a mammoth release clause of £428 million – the joint-third highest at the club behind Messi and Antoine Griezmann. He's already two years into that deal, but has said in the past that his dream is to retire at his boyhood club – so we should see Alba in a Barcelona shirt until at least 2024!

FACTPACK

Position: Left-back

Country: Spain

D.O.B: 21/03/1989

Height: 5ft 7in

Boots: adidas Copa

stagram: @jordialbaoficial

CREATE A BARCA MASCOT!

BARCELONA are one of a few La Liga teams without an official club mascot – and we think they're missing a trick! Take a look at some of the wacky mascots in Spain, then create one for the Catalan club!

MR. ~~BAR~~CELONA?

TOP TRICKSTER?

COOLEST BOOTS?

BONKERS HAIRCUT?

BAFTA AWARDS 2021

VOTE NOW!

VOTE NOW!

MATCH introduces the first-ever 'BAFTA' awards – no, not those ones! Feast your eyes on the 'Barcelona Awards For Tremendous Achievement' – then vote for your favourites for the chance to win a jaw-dropping gaming bundle!

ALL-TIME LEGEND?

GREATEST GOAL?

BEST KIT?

YOUTH PROSPECT?

GOALKEEPERS

Barca have had some super solid shot-stoppers – Andoni Zubizarreta was the first goalie to captain a side to CL glory, Victor Valdes has won more trophies than any Barca keeper, and Claudio Bravo has kept the most league clean sheets in a single season!

THE SHORTLIST
Claudio Bravo
Antoni Ramallets
Marc-Andre ter Stegen
Victor Valdes
Andoni Zubizarreta
OTHER: Write on your Form!

Valdes

FULL-BACKS

Are you going to go for two technical defenders like Gianluca Zambrotta and Giovanni van Bronckhorst, two beasts like Lilian Thuram and Eric Abidal, or a pair of attacking full-backs like Jordi Alba, Dani Alves, Sergi Barjuan and Albert Ferrer?

THE SHORTLIST
Eric Abidal
Jordi Alba
Dani Alves
Lilian Thuram
Gianluca Zambrotta
OTHER: Write on your Form!

Abidal

CENTRE-BACKS

CB warrior Carles Puyol and classy baller Gerard Pique formed one of the best defensive partnerships MATCH has ever seen, but Rafael Marquez, Javier Mascherano and Ronald Koeman were defenders who could boss midfields too!

THE SHORTLIST
Ronald Koeman
Rafael Marquez
Javier Mascherano
Gerard Pique
Carles Puyol
OTHER: Write on your Form!

Puyol

CENTRAL MIDFIELDERS

Throughout history, Barca have dominated possession through their incredible midfield talents, so good luck picking just three! As well as the shortlisted players, don't forget the likes of Luis Enrique, Deco and Yaya Toure!

THE SHORTLIST
Sergio Busquets
Johan Cruyff
Pep Guardiola
Andres Iniesta
Xavi
OTHER: Write on your Form!

Iniesta

WINGERS

MATCH thinks you're going to tear your hair out picking between Leo Messi and Diego Maradona on the right wing, and Neymar and Ronaldinho on the left – and don't forget that Thierry Henry and Marc Overmars need to be considered as well!

THE SHORTLIST
Diego Maradona
Lionel Messi
Neymar
Pedro
Ronaldinho
OTHER: Write on your Form!

Ronaldinho

FORWARDS

Having to pick just one Barcelona striker is the impossible job, so we're glad it's you that has to do it! They've had some deadly goal machines, like those shortlisted, but don't forget Patrick Kluivert, Romario and Hristo Stoichkov, either!

THE SHORTLIST
Samuel Eto'o
Rivaldo
Ronaldo
Luis Suarez
David Villa
OTHER: Write on your Form!

Villa

2 ALL-TIME LEGEND

Maradona

Now you've seen some of the best players ever to wear the famous Barcelona Blaugrana stripes, we want you to pick the club's all-time footy legend – from any superstar that's retired! Who had the biggest impact at the club?

THE SHORTLIST

Johan Cruyff

Samuel Eto'o

Pep Guardiola

Ronald Koeman

Diego Maradona

Carles Puyol

Rivaldo

Ronaldinho

Ronaldo

Victor Valdes

David Villa

Xavi

OTHER: Write on your form!

3 BEST GOAL

Messi v Athletic Bilbao

You're probably going to have to head over to YouTube to help choose the winner of this award! Check out all of the shortlisted net-busters, but feel free to pick a different one if there was a goal from this season or last that you enjoyed!

THE SHORTLIST

Andres Iniesta v Chelsea, 2009

Lionel Messi v Athletic Bilbao, 2015

Lionel Messi v Getafe, 2007

Rivaldo v Valencia, 2001

Ronaldinho v Chelsea, 2005

OTHER: Write on your form!

4 GREATEST VICTORY

Deportivo 0-8 Barcelona

There have been some really special wins over the years for Barcelona, but which was your favourite? Do you love a victory over huge rivals Real Madrid, or prefer one that helped the club lift a title? Or what about that famous CL comeback v PSG?

THE SHORTLIST

Barcelona 3-1 Man. United, 2011

Barcelona 6-1 PSG, 2017

Deportivo 0-8 Barcelona, 2016

Juventus 1-3 Barcelona, 2015

Real Madrid 2-3 Barcelona, 2017

OTHER: Write on your form!

5 BONKERS HAIRCUT

Dani Alves

You could travel back to the 1950s, '60s and '70s and find some absolutely shocking styles, but we've gone for more modern horror haircuts – these players should have known better! Which one is your favourite wacky Barcelona style?

THE SHORTLIST

Dani Alves' crazy poo emoji
Carles Puyol's caveman barnet
Lionel Messi's blond bombshell
Neymar's curly locks
Arturo Vidal's Mohawk
OTHER: Write on your form!

6 COOLEST KIT

Home 2014-15

There have been some absolute beauties over the years, but we want to crown Barca's best ever kit! Are you going for one of Nike's strips since 1998, or one of the earlier styles designed by Kappa or Meyba? For more ideas, check out pages 42–43!

THE SHORTLIST

Home 1973-74
Away 1974-75
Away 1996-97
Away 2013-14
Home 2014-15
OTHER: Write on your form!

7 BEST LA MASIA PRODUCT

Guardiola

Barcelona's youth academy is widely recognised as one of the best in the world – if not THE best! It has produced some of the greatest players ever, but who do you think is the best overall?

THE SHORTLIST

Sergio Busquets
Pep Guardiola
Andres Iniesta
Lionel Messi
Carles Puyol
Xavi
OTHER: Write on your form!

8 BEST YOUTH PROSPECT

Fati

You've picked your favourite all-time player to graduate from La Masia, now it's time to choose who you think is the best Under-21 player at the club right now! Head to page 54 for our insight into some of the club's current young ballers!

THE SHORTLIST

Hiroki Abe
Ansu Fati
Ilaix Moriba
Pedri
Riqui Puig
OTHER: Write on your form!

9 MR. BARCELONA

Xavi

This award goes to the player who best represents the club – it's got to be a fans' favourite who really understood what it means to play for Barcelona, and always respected their 'Mes Que Un Club' motto! Which superstar gets your vote?

THE SHORTLIST

Johan Cruyff

Pep Guardiola

Andres Iniesta

Carles Puyol

Xavi

OTHER: Write on your form!

10 BEST BOOTS

Neymar Nike Ousadia Alegria

The likes of Lionel Messi, Neymar, Antoine Griezmann and Ronaldinho have all received their own signature boots while playing for Barcelona, but we want you to decide which cool kicks should be top of the pile! Go...

THE SHORTLIST

Griezmann 10-Year Puma Future

Messi 15-Year adidas Nemeziz

Messi Team Mode adidas Nemeziz

Neymar Nike Ousadia Alegria

Ronaldinho Nike Tiempo Legend

OTHER: Write on your form!

'11 GREATEST TRICKSTER

Rivaldo

We want to celebrate the best Barcelona trick machine in the club's history... the player who wowed the Blaugrana crowd – and sometimes even the opposition supporters – with his quick feet, outrageous tekkers or demon dribbling!

THE SHORTLIST

Diego Maradona

Lionel Messi

Neymar

Rivaldo

Ronaldinho

OTHER: Write on your form!

'12 BEST FEMENI STAR

Hermoso

The Barcelona Femeni side won last season's league title, so we want you to pick the best player currently at the club! Turn to page 58 right now to read some sick stats from their 2019-20 standout season to help you out!

THE SHORTLIST

Caroline Graham Hansen

Jennifer Hermoso

Lieke Martens

Asisat Oshoala

Alexia Putellas

OTHER: Write on your form!

VOTE NOW!

AND YOU COULD WIN AN EPIC GAMING BUNDLE!

nacon

EPOS

For the chance to win this mind-blowing prize – which includes an awesome EPOS Sennheiser GSP 300 gaming headset and NACON REVOLUTION Pro Controller 3 for PlayStation 4 – just fill in this form with your votes, add your contact details and email a photograph to: match.magazine@kelsey.co.uk before January 31, 2021!

GOALKEEPER

FULL-BACK	CENTRE-BACK	CENTRE-BACK	FULL-BACK

MIDFIELDER	MIDFIELDER	MIDFIELDER

WINGER	FORWARD	WINGER

---

2. ALL-TIME LEGEND	8. BEST YOUTH PROSPECT
3. BEST GOAL	9. MR. BARCELONA
4. GREATEST VICTORY	10. BEST BOOTS
5. BONKERS HAIRCUT	11. GREATEST TRICKSTER
6. COOLEST KIT	12. BEST FEMENI STAR
7. BEST LA MASIA PRODUCT	

CLOSING DATE: JANUARY 31, 2021

NAME:

DATE OF BIRTH:

ADDRESS:

POSTCODE:

MOBILE:

EMAIL:

CALL YOURSELF A CULE?

Complete these Cule challenges, then tick each box once you've done them!

CULE CHALLENGE 1 ☐

Perfect the Cruyff turn!

Johan Cruyff was, and still is, a total Barcelona legend – and awesome skill move 'The Cruyff Turn' is named after him! Practise it in the garden or your local park, and film yourself once you've totally nailed it!

CULE CHALLENGE 2 ☐

Get snapped in a Barcelona shirt!

Being a Barcelona supporter, we're guessing you own at least one of the club's classic shirts from over the years! Take a picture of yourself wearing it and send it to MATCH via Facebook, Instagram or email!

CULE CHALLENGE 3 ☐

Put a Barcelona poster on your wall!

Every week MATCH has loads of posters in the magazine, so look out for one with a Barcelona superstar and make sure you stick it on your wall! If you have any special requests, get in touch!

CULE CHALLENGE 4 ☐

Beat Real Madrid on your fave video game!

It doesn't matter if you prefer FIFA or eFootball Pro Evolution Soccer, or own an Xbox or PlayStation, we just want you to set up a match against Real Madrid and beat them by at least three goals!

CULE CHALLENGE 5 ☐

Learn the Barcelona hymn!

The Barcelona hymn is sung before and after every home game, so we reckon you need to learn the tune before you get to a game in the future! Search for it on YouTube to hear the fans blast it out!

Barcelona Fans are known as Cules, Blaugranas or Azulgranas! The last two mean 'Blue and Maroon' – like the Famous club colours – while Cules means 'Bums'! If you didn't know already, that comes from when fans would sit on the walls around the Nou Camp, with their bottoms hanging over the edge!

At matches, you'll often hear fans shout 'Visca Barca' – which basically translates to 'Come on Barca'!

41

ICONIC KITS!

We look back at some of the Spanish side's standout strips through the years – and what makes them so special!

HOME **2014-15**

Barca put a poll on their website in 2019 asking fans to vote for their fave home kit from the previous decade – and this was the winner! We can't say for sure, but it might have something to do with it being the strip they won the treble in... along with Lionel Messi, Neymar and Luis Suarez scoring 122 goals in all comps – the most prolific strikeforce in Spanish footy history at the time!

AWAY **2013-14**

Barcelona's 2012-13 faded orange and yellow away kit is ranked among the worst the club has ever worn, but Nike clawed back a lot of respect when they released this strip the following year! The red and yellow stripes represent the flag of the Catalan region, which was a big deal for Blaugrana fans that had been waiting to see that particular pattern on a Barca shirt for a long time!

AWAY **2011-12**

Don't be fooled, this season's ultra-cool blackout away strip isn't Barcelona's first black kit! The colour made its debut on a Barcelona strip way back in 2011 – and it got a really good response from the supporters! The only thing they weren't convinced about was the sponsor – it was the first season in the club's history that they had a paid sponsor on both the home and away shirts!

HOME **1973-74**

As well as being before the days of having a whacking big shirt sponsor in the middle, this was also the classic kit that Netherlands baller Johan Cruyff wore in his first season at the Camp Nou, where he'd go on to leave a legendary legacy! He scored one of the best goals of his career during this season too – just search 'Cruyff's Impossible Goal' on YouTube to see what we're on about!

AWAY 1991-92

This was the shirt in which Barcelona beat Italian giants Sampdoria in their first-ever Champions League final, known back then as the European Cup. Being bright orange, just like the Netherlands' home strips, it was a cracking coincidence that the winner of the final was scored in extra-time by Dutch defender Ronald Koeman!

HOME 1982-92

You might not have heard of them, but Barca-based brand Meyba is a big deal in the city – they produced one of the club's best home kits! In fact, it was so popular, they decided to keep the same design for almost a decade! On top of that, it was also worn by total football legend Diego Maradona during his spell there!

AWAY 1974-75

Another quality kit worn by Cruyff was this yellow away one. It always stands out in fans' minds because of the dashing sash that diagonally crossed the shirt, and the way they managed to incorporate all of the important Cule colours – the yellow base, striped red armband and the Blaugrana sash and sleeves. Class!

AWAY 1996-97

There was a period of six years where Kappa produced Barcelona's strips – and this terrific teal effort was the pick of the bunch! It also happened to be worn by Brazilian net-buster Ronaldo in his jaw-dropping 47-goal season at the club, and has become such an iconic kit that Nike attempted to do their own take on it in their 2019-20 third strip!

HOME 1999-00

La Blaugrana's first shirt in history was half red and half blue, so to celebrate the club's 100th birthday in 1999, Nike designed this blast from the past! It was decorated in the middle with the years either side of the club crest and with the Nike Swoosh sitting stylishly below – not to mention being worn by the likes of Rivaldo, Kluivert, Xavi and Puyol!

HOME 2019-20

In 2015-16, Nike ditched the club's traditional vertical pattern for the first time ever on a Barcelona home shirt, opting instead for hoops, but it didn't go down very well with the fans! The mega sports brand took another risk last season with this chequered look, but its popularity was, again, mixed to say the least!

BARCELONA'S TOP 10
EL CLASICO MOMENTS!

We reveal the biggest moments and matches from BARCELONA's fierce rivalry with REAL MADRID!

Barcelona 5 Real Madrid 0
November 29th, 2010

This match came right in the middle of Pep Guardiola's incredible reign as boss, when the club were at their peak and playing teams off the park every week – including Real! They destroyed their rivals, scoring four goals in under an hour, but the match is remembered for Gerard Pique mockingly holding up five fingers towards the supporters in celebration after the last goal!

9

Real Madrid 1 Barcelona 2
April 25th, 2004

There's nothing sweeter than a late winner... especially when it's against your fiercest rivals, in their stadium and with an outrageous assist and finish! It was 1-1 in the 86th minute, when Ronaldinho scooped an epic pass over the Real defence onto an onrushing Xavi, who then acrobatically lobbed the keeper first time!

Real Madrid 0 Barcelona 2
April 27th, 2011

6

In the same season of that 5-0 thrashing, the sides later met each other four times in less than a month! This was the third clash of four – and the first leg of the Champions League semis. It was a bad-tempered game in Madrid and was heading for a goalless draw, until Barca took control with two Messi goals in 11 minutes, including a sick solo effort from a run that started almost on the halfway line!

8

Barcelona 5 Real Madrid 1
October 28th, 2018

With Cristiano Ronaldo having moved to Juventus the previous summer and Lionel Messi fracturing his arm a week before, this was the first Clasico in 11 years not to feature either of the two superstars! Would it be as exciting and dramatic? Of course it would! Luis Suarez stepped up to the plate by scoring a hat-trick, while Pique pulled out his five-finger salute once more!

7

Real Madrid 3 Barcelona 4
March 23rd, 2014

This match had everything – a Sergio Ramos red card, three penalties, crazy comebacks and a late winner! Despite Andres Iniesta putting Los Cules ahead after seven minutes, Real went 2-1 and then 3-2 up with just 30 minutes left to play! But Messi then scored two goals from the spot to bag a hat-trick, including the winner in the final minutes!

Real Madrid 0 Barcelona 5
February 17th, 1974

5

At this point in history, Real had won over twice as many La Liga titles as Barca, but La Blaugrana had a new weapon – Johan Cruyff! In his first game at the Bernabeu, he scored his first Clasico goal and led the visitors to a 5-0 thumping of Los Blancos – a result that helped Barca win their first league title in 14 years!

4

Real Madrid 2 Barcelona 2
June 26th, 1983

Something special happened in the final of the old Copa de la Liga in 1983... Diego Maradona scored an epic solo goal, dribbling round the keeper and another defender on the goal line! But it was the Bernabeu's reaction that made history – they stood and clapped his efforts! That was the first time a Cules star was applauded by Real fans, but it wouldn't be the last...

Real Madrid 2 Barcelona 6
May 2nd, 2009

3

From 2006 to 2008, Real dominated La Liga and Barca, but it all changed in 2009 after Guardiola had arrived – and this game was the proof! Real went ahead thanks to a Gonzalo Higuain strike, but three goals in either half for Pep's side secured a crushing win – and the image of club captain Carles Puyol holding up his armband is one that really sticks in fans' minds!

Real Madrid 2 Barcelona 3
April 23rd, 2017

1

This has to be No.1 for pure drama alone! Real had managed to nick a leveller in the 85th minute, despite having had Ramos sent off earlier in the game. Yet, in the last minute of stoppage-time, Sergi Roberto went on a lung-busting run up the pitch, before Messi slotted home his 500th goal for the club – which he celebrated by famously holding up his shirt towards the home supporters!

2

Real Madrid 0 Barcelona 3
November 19th, 2005

Remember what we were saying about Maradona not being the only player to be clapped by the Bernabeu? Well, here's case two – Ronaldinho! The Brazilian put on an absolute masterclass and, after scoring his second goal with more individual brilliance, the home fans had to accept his talent and rose to their feet!

ANTOINE GRIEZMANN...
ON A MISSION!

The quality BARCELONA forward chats through his epic career so far!

HIS PAST CLUBS!

ANTOINE SAYS: "I owe Real Sociedad almost everything because back then they were the only team that trusted me. They gave me all I needed to be happy on and off the pitch, and were the first team to give me a professional contract. At Atletico Madrid, it was a beautiful experience. There were moments in the dressing room, and with their fans, that were the best for me!"

SIGNING FOR BARCELONA!

ANTOINE SAYS: "I was very happy and it gives me great pride. I'm at the biggest club in the world! I'm very happy to be here and my father is proud to see his son playing for Barcelona. I want to have my name written in golden letters in the club, and its history, so I'll keep on working hard to be an important player!"

PLAYING ALONGSIDE MESSI & SUAREZ!

ANTOINE SAYS: "He is Leo Messi, the best in the world, and it has been a pleasure to play with him! I try to look at his movements and move around when he has the ball to be able to create that link. Luis Suarez's instinct in front of goal is incredible – he doesn't need many chances to score! You can see that because every time he shoots, it's a dangerous chance or a goal!"

HOME DEBUT DELIGHT!

ANTOINE SAYS: "I tried not to put too much pressure on myself. At Atletico and Real Sociedad, I always used to go to the hotel where we'd meet up pre-game, so I had my routines and everything was very different. But I'm confident and I was lucky enough to score a couple of goals, but that's not the most important thing – I just want to do my best to help my team-mates!"

SCORING AT THE CAMP NOU!

ANTOINE SAYS: "It's really great. I had a blast! I am eager to score more goals and I was waiting for the moment to come for a long time, because as a visitor I hadn't managed to score at the Camp Nou. But now I've done so wearing the Barcelona shirt and I am very, very happy!"

SETTING TARGETS!

ANTOINE SAYS: "As a team, I think that we all have it in our minds – we want to try to win all the trophies that we can. Personally, I want to improve my game in defence, in attack... a bit of everything! I want to win La Liga, the Champions League, the Copa del Rey, the Euros, another World Cup. Many things! Also, I want to make my family, teammates and friends happy!"

PLAYING IN EL CLASICO!

ANTOINE SAYS: "It's the most important game of the year. It's a great show, the previous days on the TV are intense – I always used to watch it on TV – and we do everything we can to be at 100% to win the match. It's a game that you want to be a part of no matter how!"

SCORING v REAL!

ANTOINE SAYS: "Scoring in a game like this is always a massive source of pride, but as I said I'm not a player that just thinks about scoring. I want to do what's best for the team, whatever that might be at any given time. If I score, then it's brilliant, but I'm not going to spend the whole game shooting to score if I can be more of a help in another way!"

LaLigaTV is the only way to watch all of LaLiga, all in one place. **LaLiga** *TV*

STAT ATTACK!

Get a load of BARCA's biggest signings, mega trophy cabinet, record goalscorers, social media followers and tons more!

FIVE BIGGEST SIGNINGS

	PLAYER	YEAR	FEE
1	Antoine Griezmann	2019	£107m
2	Philippe Coutinho	2018	£105m
3	Ousmane Dembele	2017	£97m
4	Neymar	2013	£78m
5	Luis Suarez	2014	£65m

FIVE BIGGEST SALES

	PLAYER	YEAR	FEE
1	Neymar	2017	£198m
2	Arthur	2020	£65m
3	Luis Figo	2000	£37m
4	Malcom	2019	£36.6m
5	Alexis Sanchez	2014	£35m

MAJOR TROPHIES

5	Champions League
3	FIFA Club World Cup
4	European Cup Winners' Cup
3	Fairs Cup
5	UEFA Super Cup
26	La Liga
30	Copa del Rey
13	Spanish Super Cup

ALL-TIME TOP SCORERS

Player	Years	Goals
Lionel Messi	2004-	633
Cesar	1942-1955	232
Luis Suarez	2014-	196
Laszlo Kubala	1950-1961	194
Josep Samitier	1919-1932	184
Josep Escola	1934-1949	167
Paulino Alcantara	1912-16 & 1918-27	143
Samuel Eto'o	2004-2009	130
Rivaldo	1997-2002	130
Mariano Martin	1940-1948	128

9

In 2013-14, Pedro scored the fastest hat-trick in Barcelona history! He smashed in three goals in just nine first-half minutes against Getafe!

CHAMPIONS LEAGUE RECORD
ALL-TIME

PLAYED 255

WON 150

LOST 43

DRAWN 62

GOALS 512

CONCEDED 246

ALL-TIME APPEARANCE MAKERS

Guillermo Amor 421

Carles Rexach 449

Xavi 767

Victor Valdes 535

Gerard Pique 541

Lionel Messi 729

Migueli 549

Andres Iniesta 674

Sergio Busquets 578

Carles Puyol 593

Barcelona's 100 points from the 2012-13 campaign is a joint-record high for a single La Liga season!

100

11 COUNTRIES REPRESENTED IN 2019-20 SQUAD

 Portugal

 Spain

 Croatia

 France

 Germany

 Brazil

 Uruguay

Argentina

 Netherlands

 Chile

 Denmark

BIGGEST VICTORIES

LA LIGA HOME
10-1
v Gimnastic de Tarragona, 1949

LA LIGA AWAY
0-8
v Deportivo, 2016*

*Also beat three other teams 8-0 away

facebook
103m+
LIKES

Instagram
87m+
FOLLOWERS

twitter
59m+
FOLLOWERS

Stats only include official matches. Correct up to end of 2019-20 La Liga season.

SPOT THE DIFFERENCE

Study these Barcelona v Athletic Bilbao pictures very carefully, then see if you can find the ten differences between them!

NAME THE TEAM

Can you remember the superstars that lined up in Barcelona's 3-1 win over Borussia Dortmund in last season's CL clash?

1. Goalkeeper

3. Centre-back

5. Midfielder

2. Centre-back

4. Left-back

6. Midfielder

7. Forward

9. Forward

11. Striker

8. Right-back

10. Midfielder

ANSWERS ON PAGE 60

ANSU FATI
WONDERKID WINGER

Last season saw the talent emerge from the academy shadows

Ansu Fati has received plenty of praise since making his Barcelona debut in August 2019, but being singled out by Leo Messi is undoubtedly a little bit more special than the rest. "He got my attention from the first time I saw him in training. He has the potential to be a very important player, but we have to help him, " Messi said after winning his record-breaking sixth Ballon d'Or award. It's that incredible potential that has seen the youngster's meteoric rise from exciting academy prospect to a first team player – and with his pace, direct running and ability to find a teammate with his final ball, it should only be a matter of time before he's one of the first names on the Blaugrana teamsheet...

CLASICO SHOWDOWN

Fati's family moved to Spain when he was just six years old, but by the age of eight he was already ripping it up for Sevilla's academy! Before long, scouts from Barcelona and Real Madrid were making regular trips to watch him play – and it was Real who made the first move! They offered more money for Fati to join the capital club, but it was Barca's La Masia academy and residency that convinced the youngster to head there instead when he was just ten!

RECORD BREAKER

In August 2019, Fati became the youngest-ever player to feature for the first team in the league at 16 years and 298 days old! In fact, he was so young, Barca needed his parents' permission for him to make his debut! The records didn't stop there, though – a week later he became Barca's youngest player to score in La Liga, in September he became their youngest star in the Champions League, and in December he became the youngest goalscorer in CL history!

SPAIN SUPERSTAR

Even though he was born in Guinea-Bissau, Africa, and could've represented Portugal, Fati's spent most of his life in Spain and gained Spanish citizenship in September 2019. He was called up to the Spain Under-21 team a month later, and made his debut against Montenegro that same month. With the 2020 European Championship pushed back to the summer of 2021, the winger's got a real chance of breaking into the senior squad and making it on to the plane!

CURRENT CONTRACT

After breaking into the first team, Barca's bosses realised they needed to stop other clubs from sniffing around their wonderkid. They handed Fati a new contract in December 2019, which runs until 2022, with the possibility to extend until 2024. Barcelona also raised his release clause from €100 million to €170 million, although that will increase to €400 million as soon as he turns 18! Basically, Los Cules want to make him untouchable to other clubs!

FACTPACK

Position: Winger
Country: Spain
D.O.B: 31/10/2002
Height: 5ft 8in
Boots: Nike Mercurial
Instagram: @ansufati

TURN OVER FOR MORE BARCA WONDERKIDS!

BARCA'S NEXT GENERATION!

We take a closer look at five of the hottest young talents who are ready to make a name for themselves at the Nou Camp over the next few years!

POTENTIAL
8
/10

RONALD ARAUJO
Centre-Back

The Uruguay defender's Barca debut was a total nightmare – he was sent off 13 minutes after coming on as a sub back in October 2019! He's proved since that he's got the tackling and technical abilities to be a top player!

TOP SKILL: **Awareness**

POTENTIAL
9
/10

RIQUI PUIG
Midfielder

The classy midfielder joined La Masia when he was 14, and has been ranked as one of the club's best young prospects ever since! His footy brain, passing and vision could see him develop into the next Xavi!

TOP SKILL: **Passing**

PEDRI
Winger

The teenager was playing first-team football for Las Palmas when he was just 16 years old! Barcelona agreed a deal to sign him last summer, with his release clause rising to £328 million as soon as he plays for the first team!

TOP SKILL: **Dribbling**

POTENTIAL
9
/10

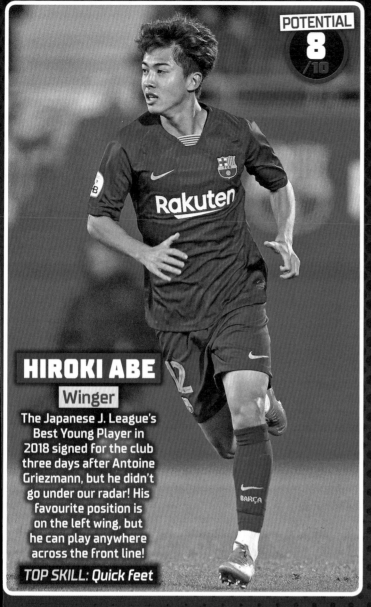

HIROKI ABE

Winger

The Japanese J. League's Best Young Player in 2018 signed for the club three days after Antoine Griezmann, but he didn't go under our radar! His favourite position is on the left wing, but he can play anywhere across the front line!

TOP SKILL: *Quick feet*

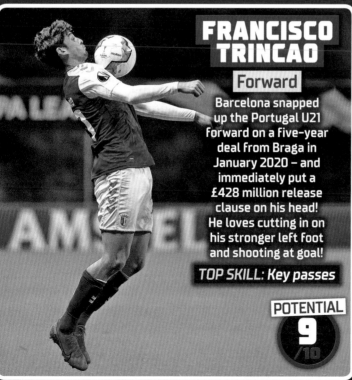

FRANCISCO TRINCAO

Forward

Barcelona snapped up the Portugal U21 forward on a five-year deal from Braga in January 2020 – and immediately put a £428 million release clause on his head! He loves cutting in on his stronger left foot and shooting at goal!

TOP SKILL: *Key passes*

POTENTIAL
9
/10

BARCELONA'S FORGOTTEN MEN!

We've picked out five players you might not remember actually came through the club's famous La Masia academy...

Mauro Icardi

The PSG striker spent two-and-a-half seasons in the youth teams at the start of Pep Guardiola's time in charge of the club!

Andre Onana

The Cameroon goalkeeper joined Barcelona's academy as part of club legend Samuel Eto'o's Foundation, but was snapped up by Ajax a few years later!

Adama Traore

The take-on machine has developed into the player Barcelona hoped he would have been when he was on their books as a youngster!

Alex Grimaldo

The left-back was the youngest-ever player to star in the Segunda Division when he made his Barca B debut at 15, but then he joined Benfica!

Keita Balde

Even though he's played 30 times for Senegal, the forward was born in Catalonia and spent seven years in Barca's youth teams!

2020-21 HOME SHIRT

We take a closer look at BARCA's stunning 2020-21 home threads...

The yellow pinstripes are inspired by the club's classic crest from their golden period back in the 1920s!

As well as ditching the chequered pattern to return to their traditional stripes, Barca have also reverted back to a rounded collar!

New signing Miralem Pjanic, who joined the club from Juventus for £54 million, will be mega keen to impress in the quality kit!

The slick shirt also takes inspiration from another more recent season – the mega successful 2010-11 campaign! See below...

WINNING VIBES!

Check out the similarity between their new kit and this bad boy from a decade ago! Can they repeat its success?

Spanish Super Cup!

Barcelona started 2010-11 with a bang, coming back from a 3-1 first-leg deficit to hammer Sevilla 4-0 in the Spanish Super Cup!

La Liga!

Barca won their third straight title under Pep Guardiola, as they finished four points above mega rivals Real Madrid!

Champions League!

Los Cules completed a class campaign with a 3-win over Man. United in the Champions League final at Wembley!

MEET THE MANAGER

RONALD KOEMAN

Get the complete lowdown on the gaffer in charge of BARCELONA...

HERO OF WEMBLEY!

Koeman's nickname while playing for Barcelona was 'Tintin', after the famous cartoon character, but he left as 'The Hero of Wembley'! It came after he scored the only goal of the 1992 European Cup final, from a fine free-kick at Wembley against Sampdoria, to make the club European champions for the first time in its history. Legend!

LEGEND RETURNS!

The Dutch manager is a real icon at Barcelona! He joined the Spanish side as a player from PSV in 1989, and went on to win four league titles during his six-year spell at the club. He was a midfielder who mainly played as a centre-back, so he had great technical ability on the ball and a real eye for goal – he scored 88 times for the club!

"Everyone knows that Barcelona is my dream club. It feels very special to me to be able to become a coach there!"
Ronald Koeman, Barcelona coach

DUTCH DNA!

In the likes of Koeman and Johan Cruyff, Barca have had some great Dutch players through their history! The club still have high hopes for central midfielder Frenkie de Jong, and fans will be hoping Koeman will be able to bring the best out of him – the manager gave de Jong his senior international debut for the Netherlands back in 2018!

LEGENDS LINK-UP!

Koeman wasn't the only legend to return to the club in the summer of 2020! Ex-striker Henrik Larsson, who played with Koeman when they were both at Feyenoord, signed a two-year deal to work as the team's assistant coach. The former Sweden goal grabber spent two years at Barcelona and won back-to-back La Liga titles!

STAT ATTACK!

We take a closer look at some of Koeman's best Barca stats...

2
When Koeman moved to the Camp Nou back in 1989, he became the club's second-most expensive signing in history!

264
He played 264 times in all competitions for Barcelona during his six-year spell, including 192 games in La Liga. Wow!

10
He won ten trophies as a player during his stint at the club, including three Spanish Super Cups, the Copa del Rey and UEFA Super Cup!

5
He scored five goals against arch-rivals Real Madrid in a Blaugrana shirt, making him a real fans' favourite!

FEMENI CHAMPS!

Even though the season couldn't be completed, BARCELONA FEMENI were awarded the 2019-20 league title on a points-per-game basis! We take a look at some of their best stats from last campaign...

21 — They were unbeaten in 21 matches before the season was cancelled – winning 19 and drawing the other two games!

13 — Their incredible streak of 13 victories on the bounce was the longest winning run of the season!

86 — They'd busted 86 nets in 21 games – averaging just over four goals a game. Lethal!

4 — Goalkeeper Sandra Panos won her fourth Zamora Trophy – for the least goals-per-game conceded – after letting in just five goals!

9 They were nine points above second-placed Atletico Madrid by the time the season ended!

5 The 2019-20 league title was the club's fifth in history – and their first since 2014-15!

23 Deadly striker Jennifer Hermoso finished the season as top goalscorer with 23 net-busters!

6 They were just as strong in defence – they only conceded six goals all season!

10 They were involved in the highest-scoring game of the season – beating Real Madrid-owned CD Tacon 9-1!

QUIZ ANSWERS

Brain-Buster P16

1. Valencia
2. True
3. Real Sociedad
4. Green
5. Barcelona 0-2 Real Madrid
6. 2014
7. Andres Iniesta
8. Middlesbrough
9. Luis Suarez
10. Older

Wordfit P17

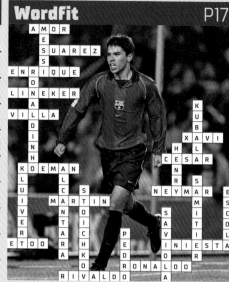

Action Replay P31

1. October
2. Rafinha
3. Philippe Coutinho
4. False – Suarez's first goal was a penalty
5. Barcelona 2-0 Real Madrid
6. Marcelo
7. His head
8. Real Madrid
9. True

Wordsearch P30

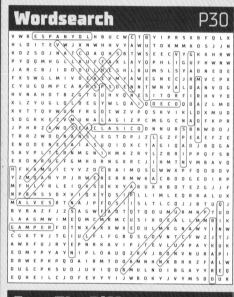

Name The Team P51

1. Marc-Andre ter Stegen
2. Samuel Umtiti
3. Clement Lenglet
4. Junior Firpo
5. Ivan Rakitic
6. Sergio Busquets
7. Lionel Messi
8. Sergi Roberto
9. Ousmane Dembele
10. Frenkie de Jong
11. Luis Suarez

Spot The Difference P50

SUBSCRIBE TO MATCH! & GET THIS EPIC GIFT!*

AWESOME BOOMPODS SPEAKER WORTH £34.99!

2 PACKS OF ADRENALYN XL!

SAVE OVER 30% ON THE SHOP PRICE!

PACKED EVERY WEEK WITH...

★ Cool gear & quizzes

★ FIFA tips & stats

★ Footy LOLs & more!

HOW TO SUBSCRIBE TO MATCH!

CALL
01959 543 747
QUOTE: MATAN21

ONLINE
SHOP.KELSEY.CO.UK/ MATAN21

ROLL OF HONOUR

CHAMPIONS LEAGUE
1991-92, 2005-06, 2008-09, 2010-11, 2014-15

FIFA CLUB WORLD CUP
2009, 2011, 2015

EUROPEAN CUP WINNERS' CUP
1978-79, 1981-82, 1988-89, 1996-97

FAIRS CUP
1957-58, 1959-60, 1965-66 (won outright in 1971)

EUROPEAN SUPER CUP
1992, 1997, 2009, 2011, 2015

LA LIGA
1928-29, 1944-45, 1947-48, 1948-49, 1951-52, 1952-53,
1958-59, 1959-60, 1973-74, 1984-85, 1990-91, 1991-92,
1992-93, 1993-94, 1997-98, 1998-99, 2004-05, 2005-06,
2008-09, 2009-10, 2010-11, 2012-13, 2014-15, 2015-16,
2017-18, 2018-19

COPA DEL REY
1909-10, 1911-12, 1912-13, 1919-20, 1921-22, 1924-25, 1925-26,
1927-28, 1941-42, 1950-51, 1951-52, 1952-53, 1956-57, 1958-59,
1962-63, 1967-68, 1970-71, 1977-78, 1980-81, 1982-83,
1987-88, 1989-90, 1996-97, 1997-98, 2008-09,
2011-12, 2014-15, 2015-16, 2016-17, 2017-18

SPANISH SUPER CUP
1983, 1991, 1992, 1994, 1996, 2005, 2006, 2009,
2010, 2011, 2013, 2016, 2018

SPANISH LEAGUE CUP
1982-83, 1985-86

SMALL WORLD CUP
1957

LATIN CUP
1949, 1952

PYRENEES CUP
1910, 1911, 1912, 1913

MEDITERRANEAN LEAGUE
1937

CATALAN LEAGUE
1937-38

CATALAN LEAGUE CHAMPIONSHIP
1901-02, 1902-03, 1904-05, 1908-09, 1909-10, 1910-11,
1912-13, 1915-16, 1918-19, 1919-20, 1920-21, 1921-22, 1923-24,
1924-25, 1925-26, 1926-27, 1927-28, 1929-30, 1930-31,
1931-32, 1934-35, 1935-36, 1937-38 (includes Copa
Macaya 1901-02 & Copa Barcelona 1902-03)

CATALAN SUPER CUP
2014-15

CATALAN CUP
1990-91, 1992-93, 1999-2000, 2003-04, 2004-05, 2006-07,
2012-13, 2013-14 (until 1993-94, Copa Generalitat)

COPA EVA DUARTE
1948-49, 1951-52, 1952-53